MW01613294

PLUM POEMS

by Svein Myreng

PARALLAX PRESS
BERKELEY, CALIFORNIA

For mother,
Astrid Myreng (1926–1997),
in endless gratitude.
No poem without you!

✿

Parallax Press
P.O. Box 7355
Berkeley, California 94707

Cover painting, "Ways to the Heart,"
watercolor by Anna Pardini.
Cover and text design by Legacy Media, Inc.
Author photo by Candace Cassin.

Library of Congress Cataloging-in-Publication Data
Myreng, Svein.
    Plum poems / by Svein Myreng.
    p. cm.
    ISBN 1-888375-06-x (pbk.)
    1. Zen poetry, English-Norway.   1. Title.
    PR9144.9.M96 P58 1999
    821–dc21   99-24382
                                                  CIP

1 2 3 4 5 6 7 8 9 10 / 03 02 01 00 99

Contents

Foreword *by Thich Nhat Hanh*   *VII*

Publisher's Preface   *VIII*

Acceptance   *3*

Gratitude   *8*

Illumination   *9*

Celebration   *10*

First Loves   *11*

Sangha Body   *13*

A Long Enduring Mind   *15*

Tears   *18*

Summer Opening   *18*

Gathas   *19*

Gatha for the Lamp Transmission   *20*

Haiku   *20*

Manifesto   *22*

The Joy of Simplicity   *23*

Grace   *25*

For Thây   *26*

Tonight   *26*

Wood   *27*

Free   *28*

Daybreak   *28*

Space   *29*

On This Earth   *30*

Morning   *31*

Refuge   *32*

Dandelion   *32*

Sketch   *34*

Reconciling with Christianity   35
O!   39
Calm   39
A Rose   40
Snow   40
Sadness and the Sky   42
The Joy of Walking Fast   43
Still, Alive   47
Mindfulness of the Body   48
In the Japanese Garden   52
Mother   53
Astrid Myreng,
   Source of Courageous Engagement   55
POEMS FOR EEVI
      For You   57
      Our Path   58
      Joy   60
      Today   61

Foreword

These poems stem from many years' practice of
mindfulness, peace, and joy, in Plum Village and
in Norway. The poet, Svein Myreng, a friend
and student of mine, first came to Plum Village
in 1989, and has returned to practice with the
Sangha there year after year. Having deep love
for the Buddha's teachings, he also stays rooted
in his own background. This lets his practice
and poems be informed by the great literature,
poetry, and traditional Norwegian culture and
nature that he loves so much.

Being born with a delicate heart, a congeni-
tal heart disease, Svein has looked deeply into
illness, suffering, and the impermanent nature of
all that is, and his insight makes him live very
intensely, very mindfully. It also helps him
appreciate the miracle of ordinary experiences,
like the sky, the trees, a friend's smile.

His poems reflect this insight and joy. They
can be a source of inspiration to many of us in
our continued practice of the Dharma.

> Thich Nhat Hanh
> Plum Village, France
> March 1999

Publisher's Preface

Svein Myreng lives in Oslo, Norway, with his beloved wife Eevi Beck. He was born with a congenital heart disease, which brought him close to illness and death from early on, and taught him to appreciate what is really important in life. An existential crisis when he was in his early twenties, with desperate questioning about the meaning of life, and a strong fear of death, brought him in contact with the Buddha's teaching. In 1997, major heart surgery at Children's Hospital in Boston gave him more strength and physical well-being than he has ever had — beginning a new phase in his life.

In 1987, he met Thich Nhat Hanh and Sister Chân Không when they visited Norway, and he first visited Plum Village one and a half years later. Getting into a gentler, more everyday-focused practice than the Rinzai Zen he had practiced so far, gave a new orientation to his life, and brought to blossom many values from his "pre-Zen-life." In 1990, he met his other great Buddhist influence, Bhante Sumanaratana from Sri Lanka, at that time abbot of Stockholm Buddhist Vihara in Sweden. (Bhante has since disrobed, and is at the moment a Ph.D. student at Oxford University.)

He has practiced Dharma with teachers from

the Zen and Theravada traditions, primarily Ven. Dhyana Master Thich Nhat Hanh and his students, and Dhamma teacher Bhante Sumanaratana. Svein is a Dharmacharya in the Order of Interbeing.

He also works as a teacher of Norwegian as a second language, to refugees and immigrants to Norway. Meeting students from many continents and cultures continues to inspire him.

Many of these poems have been written in Plum Village, inspired by — and in gratitude to — the joy, love, and transformation he has experienced there. This is Svein's first collection of poems. He never thought his poems were good enough for publication like this, but was strongly encouraged by Thich Nhat Hanh to gather them into a collection.

PLUM POEMS

Acceptance

I was born with a congenital heart disease that
has limited my physical activity and more than
once has brought me to the brink of death.
Mental aspects of this handicap have, on the
whole, been hardest to handle. The gap between
my wish to be active and the limits set by my
heart condition has been difficult at times, but
the feeling that my disability made me worth-
less has been the real problem. I don't know
how early in life this feeling started to grow, or
why, but I think it has been with me for a long
time. It probably was nourished by other
people's fear and denial about disease and
handicaps, and their aversion to suffering. In my
teens, this feeling grew into a wish to hide my
heart completely and to restrain my breath
carefully, never to sound out-of-breath. I fought
hard to pretend that all was well. Carrying my
"dark secret," it has taken me many years of
meditation to open up.

I believe this is a universal experience. The
pressures from society's expectations and hopes
— other people's as well as our own — shape us
into patterns that do not fit. Our healthy emo-
tional tissue gets scarred by all the cosmetic
surgery that is performed on our mind.

After meeting Thây, it became clear to me
that practicing acceptance is essential for heal-

ing. Acceptance is not fatalistic passivity where we believe that we just have to endure. Acceptance is to acknowledge a situation for what it is and to calm down inside of it. If we then find we can bring about change, very good! If not, then we must acknowledge and accept that. In both cases, a clear, open heart and mind are useful.

Recently I woke up with my heart beating extremely fast and out of rhythm. Though unpleasant physically, I noticed that I didn't feel the strong sense of failure that this illness has triggered in me in the past. I was able to stay calm and reasonably happy, dwelling in the present moment. This felt very satisfying and has given me further trust in mindfulness practice. It also showed that acceptance is very close to patience. Physical or mental pain often brings a burning sense of restlessness. When we can stay aware and not be carried away by it, we can be present and not make things worse by futile attempts to escape that only bring tension and conflict.

Even more useful than accepting difficult situations is accepting our own reactions to them. When our feelings and thoughts are not calm and patient, but rather angry, jealous, or petty, they are often difficult to accept. Our self-image is threatened. It is helpful to remember that thoughts and feelings arise naturally. The question is how we react to them.

The Buddha mentions three ways of reacting that create difficulties. One is escaping from an unpleasant situation into sensual pleasures or fantasy through entertainment, food, sex, or shopping. We lose important opportunities to learn how to cope with difficulties and easily become victims of the many toxins in modern culture. The second way is to cling to experiences. As everything changes, this attitude also removes us from the way things are. The third is to try to block off large parts of ourselves. With concentration, we can become aware of these habits, and they will no longer dominate us. Practicing acceptance, we can allow more of our imperfections to be visible. We can learn more about ourselves and walk more lightly through life. This also makes us more tolerant of others. We won't need to project our dark sides onto others, and we become more open-minded.

Accepting and seeing ever more subtle feelings, thoughts, and impulses can be quite a challenge. I sense how I'd like to be perfect and tend not to allow myself much leeway. I can see that both the thirst for situations to go away and the wish to be someone special bring strain and unpleasantness. Slowly, as I accept myself, I let go more and more. We can remember that our internal knots — desire, aversion, ignorance, pride, indecision — are universal. There is no need to blame ourselves for them.

If our intentions are good and honest and we are willing to use difficulties as a way to learn, the *Sutra of Assembled Treasures* has this encouraging comment: "Just as the excrement and garbage disposed by the people living in big cities will yield benefit when placed in vineyards and sugarcane fields, so the residual afflictions of a bodhisattva will yield benefits because they are conducive to all-knowing understanding." Another exercise is to celebrate imperfection instead of seeing it as something undesirable. We acknowledge that life will never be perfect and we can actually enjoy this fact!

On their first visit to Plum Village, many people have difficulties with the simple living conditions, constantly changing schedule, and lack of orderly silence. Both this situation and our reactions to it can be very valuable, as they challenge our habits and expectations. I have a hunch that this is one of the reasons why Plum Village allows people to get in touch with deep aspects of themselves so remarkably quickly. (Of course, love, beauty, and a happy atmosphere help.)

The practice of acceptance helps us attain the stillness described in *The Miracle of Mind-*

fulness: "Once your feelings and thoughts no longer disturb you, at that time mind begins to dwell in mind. Your mind will take hold of mind in a direct and wondrous way, which no longer differentiates between subject and object." We can be alive and cheerful, moving from one moment to the next, shedding our sorrows as we go.

Gratitude

I'm so grateful to have friends:
greeting with a lotus bud
two clear eyes   a smile
a comradely arm around my shoulder
a vibrant breathing hug
tears together.

I'm so grateful to be alone:
crickets in darkening grass
a walk among pine trees
be with the ocean's pulse
or the silent early dawn.

Ah! to exchange, to flow...
and to rest in the center
To walk with peace
within chaos.

Illumination

In the midst of joy and ease,
hard blows hit me:
fear, disease.

When I've come deepest down,
trees and friends and grass support me.
Great the joys we never own!

Suddenly the world is new!
When did the bell sound like this!
When was the sky this shade of blue!

But it's easy to forget,
and withdraw in sour frowns —
until suddenly I let

All get lit up by a breath!
Bee and smile and cloud are now and true.

Celebration

for the ten-year anniversary of Plum Village (1992)

I want to celebrate chaos.
I want to celebrate old worn-out cars,
broken tiles, ever-shifting
schedules, misplaced letters,
and nettles next to flower-beds;
to celebrate toilets out of order,
as well as friends who will remind me
that mistakes are good, failures a success,
and that a pure heart *may* prevail
in the non-end.
I want to celebrate being left alone,
or assailed by talkers,
(or, disturbing others' quiet).
I want to celebrate gentle smiles,
good intentions, and, *especially,*
one step after the other.
"If arrow number 100 hits the target,
how can you say the first 99 were failures?"

First Loves

Socrates was my first love.
Sitting on my grand-uncle's lap,
I was immersed in tales of
Greek and Norse gods and heroes:
escaping with Odysseus from the Cyclop's cave,
sacrificing one eye with Odin
for the gift of poetry.
But the old sage from Athens lived on in me,
as he walked the gardens with his questions,
and calmly emptied his poison cup.
Around the radio on our kitchen table
with my mother and grandmother,
we suffered with Jean Valjean in cruel times.
Our hearts glowed with dreams of justice.
And from ships on Far Eastern seas,
my father's letters came
with stories from a wondrous land,
where fortune and misfortune
couldn't always be distinguished.
The magical world of childhood!

But later, when I was fifteen or so,
the golden ball was cracked.
Its warm glow started to give way
to the cold light of neon signs
and lonely TV sets.
For many years I wandered
a land of concrete city streets,

turning my back to people
as they turned their backs to me.
My wish for love was left unexpressed,
my voice stifled and flat.
Death was there,
as a frightening black hole in my heart.
Then a door opened slightly.
An old Japanese man with mossy twigs for
eyebrows
told a secret:
"You can see. It has been done before.
The golden light is still around us."

My grand-uncle's rasping voice,
father riding distant waves,
and the safe space of grandmother and mother —
silken threads in the Norns' tapestry.
Socrates, Jean Valjean, and
Suzuki's T'ang dynasty friends —
matches lighting the candle
in the Transformation Hall.
I bow down gratefully and touch the warm
ground
of the here and now.

> Written at the Plum Village retreat of June '92, where
> Thây suggested we write about our first love — what
> were our early inspirations or even awakenings of the
> mind of love — bodhichitta.

Sangha Body

Tender grasses made me.
Summer breeze and stars made me.
A mother's gentle hands made me.
Sharp pains and fevers made me.
Noble dreams and friends' love
made me who I am.

What made you, my friend?
What were the steps
that brought you here?
Please tell me your story, friend.
Tell me your fears,
your cries for help
that no one heard,
your hopes,
and the laughter deep in your eyes.

Joining hands
in a wide circle,
we reach out together
towards the bird's clear song.
The soil, the wind,
a thousand generations' knowledge
live in your body.
In your heart,
the Sangha dreams.

Across the widest ocean
we still see each other.
Within the world's noise
we can hear the silent bell.

A Long Enduring Mind

When we take up the practice of mindfulness, it feels wonderful. We enjoy a new calm and serenity, see trees and the sky more vividly, and find pleasure in a community that values friendliness and equanimity. This is the "honeymoon" of mindfulness practice, to be enjoyed fully. But it doesn't last in this way. After a while, there usually comes a time when we are assailed by the strangest thoughts and emotions. We wonder where the precious calm of our earlier meditation periods went, and our formerly lovable Sangha friends suddenly show the most unpleasant habits. Something feels rotten in this state of Dharma.

This is a common phase in the practice, and, believe it or not, a very useful one. As mindfulness helps our mind and body relax more deeply, long repressed "internal knots" start to dissolve and surface. We become aware of subtle thoughts, impulses, and feelings that we simply didn't notice earlier. Sometimes, our practice lets us get in touch with these "hidden" aspects, while our mindfulness is not yet strong enough for us to digest them fully. We easily project feelings or character traits onto others. Also, inevitable differences in temperament and conflicting interests become visible as we get more in touch with both ourselves and our

Sangha sisters and brothers. Together, these factors can create turbulence in any Sangha, and usually, we cannot reduce them to simple questions of being right or wrong. At such times, many practitioners become deeply worried; after all, we sought peace, not a new place of conflict. Some may leave the Sangha and the practice altogether.

In 1991, I stayed in Plum Village for a few months. There were various difficulties and tensions among members of the Sangha (including me), but we knew that we had to live with each other and find ways to solve our difficulties. (Happily, there are tools, like the "Beginning Anew" ceremony.) In this process, we got to know each other and ourselves more as real people, not just on the surface, and some true friendships developed from this.

C.G. Jung coined two useful terms: The *persona* is basically our self-image, the image we present to society. The *shadow* is the hidden aspects of ourselves, the parts that we don't want to see, are unable to see, and have never really been allowed to express. It takes a great (unconscious) effort to keep the shadow in the shadow, and liberating this energy makes life a lot richer.

When we accept the difficulties of the practice and stay with our Sangha and ourselves, we shed the light of mindfulness on the shadow.

We get to know our Sangha friends on a deeper level than the persona, learning to appreciate them as real, multifaceted people. This helps us appreciate the multitude of mental factors that exist in the depths of ourselves as well. Fearless in relation to the unpleasant, we make peace within our Sangha and within ourselves. This is real maturation: moving from the concept of how we *should* be, to understanding how we *are* — changing all the time. If we leave when the Sangha honeymoon is over and search for another Sangha instead, we will never know this maturation, friendship, and deeper peace that comes through understanding and transforming difficulties. (In certain cases, though, we may have to acknowledge that a situation is really too harmful to stay in.)

As mindfulness deepens, we get more truly in touch with joy, peace, and life as a whole. I doubt that this will ever remove our difficulties completely, but it will give us a larger perspective and a deeper equanimity. I'm fond of Chinese Zen Master Xu Yun's expression, "a long enduring mind." He lived to be 120, so he should know! Even with less longevity, a long enduring mind, a passion to go more deeply, is a real gift.

Tears

Your tears in my eyes
My tears in your eyes
On this path where
joy and sorrow merge —
amazing!
Each raindrop makes a
greener leaf.

Summer Opening

for Plum Village

sweet rain falls on
the thirsty ground
                our ears
summer breeze caresses
the open landscape
                our nostrils
dandelions send down
strong roots
                our stories
strange sweet fruits
appear!
                ourselves

Gathas

Not through expectations, pride,
        or a heavy heart
do I meet the small wildflower.
But gently. Simply. And with friends' kindness.

Raindrops falling into the silent well.

Sitting on this bus,
I have limitless time.
Time to relax, breathe
and smile.

Deep within I have many tears,
        many questions.
Bringing my mind home
        10 times, 10,000 times,
will I meet the answer here?

Gatha for the Lamp Transmission

In the heart of pain and sorrow,
a tender rose grows. Water it
with clarity and kindness, friends and trees.
We'll see its sweet pale blossom open!

Haiku

On the bare branch
just one blue flower!
Summer in Plum Village

On the shiny kettle
a slender string of porridge —
early morning light

Trees in silhouette
against the red horizon —
early morning privilege

The dancing of my thoughts
swallows soar playfully
Your image

Alone this autumn evening —
sounds of voices
in the room next door

Gray, busy day
one sunray —
I'm here!

The blue sky winks
to the golden birch —
I forget my thoughts of poetry

Manifesto

I just want to
enjoy life
fly away with the
    evening breeze
hug a friend
laugh at silly jokes
shed a tear
disappear in a
    snowflake, &
be a
    happy skeleton!

The Joy of Simplicity

The great hero of Norwegian folktales, Espen the Ash Lad, got his name because he sat in front of the fireplace day in and day out. Not your most productive activity, but Espen's renowned kindness and inventiveness must have originated during these idle moments in front of the fire.

We often have an idea of time as something finite that we have to use as fully as possible while we have it. But, paradoxically, the more we fill our time with activity, the more it shrinks and disappears. Contemporary society pushes us into many frantic activities. Still, as I sit writing this on my verandah, the birds and blue sky remind me that life's greatest treasures are free. By cutting down on work, meetings, and organized activities that aren't really necessary, we give ourselves the chance to relax. Then, we can see what brings us peace and how much time we spend running away from difficulties or preserving our self-image. Our value in life doesn't depend on cleverness, what we own, or what we do, but most of us have a deep belief that these are the things that justify our existence. We need to look more deeply to get in touch with what we really enjoy and what is really good for us, and we need the courage to follow our insights.

We also need to get in touch with our lazy nature. Like Espen the Ash Lad, who spent countless hours looking into the fireplace, I have used illness to make myself stop and experience periods of inactivity. Whenever I get too caught up in busy living and ignore the signals from my body and soul, bad colds or flu take over. So I've had no choice but to be in touch with my needs, and I don't experience this so much anymore. I seem to be more lazy and energetic at the same time! A more relaxed and mindful life diminishes our energy leaks *(asrava)*, the drain that comes when our mind constantly chases ideas, desires, and projects.

The world is full of suffering, so how can we justify a lazy, relaxed lifestyle? The question is rather, in what ways do our fast lifestyles and forced activity contribute to the ills of the world? Western consumerist lifestyles lay waste to the Earth, while not bringing true happiness to anyone. The prestige carried by our culture also creates a strong incentive for materialism and injustice in poorer parts of the world. By lazily going against the stream of consumerism — and showing ways to true joy — we are doing something very useful. More relaxed and simple in our lifestyle, we may be surprised to find ourselves drawn more to give our time, energy, and material resources to beings and situations that truly need us.

Grace

There is a stillness
simpler than silence,
a peace deeper
than calm.

There is a shimmering
in dark soil,
shades of trees,
in old moss, and the twisted
forms of branches,
that hold us, carry us
and nurture us.

In a flash of the eye,
laughter, or a tear.
No effort needed, no self to seek,
just grace remains.

For Thây

In this amazing tapestry,
our lives interweave
            constantly.
Taking one step and one more,
I gently smile
to happiness and sorrow.
Alone? I must be joking!

Tonight

Tonight, I want to
write a poem
in gratitude
to these amazing things —
the family line
Thây's serious face
the night sky
deep and dark behind
soft clouds.
My tears and heartbeat,
with a tender
feeling —
Touched by the small
grains of life
we all pass on.

Wood

The image of unpolished wood
nourishes me.
A worn kitchen table
my grandfather's hands resting,
rolled-up sleeves, calm
after a day's work.
Quiet.

The smell of pine needles.
Feet moving slowly on springy
forest paths.
"I find God in the woods,"
my grandfather said —
& his parting words:
"So beautiful! Like
the fjords
& mountains of
Hardanger…"

My grandfather died young, when
I was only two years old —
but today, on this old path,
doesn't his love of the forest
give peace to my steps?

Daybreak

Moment by moment, the
dark sky shrinks.
Scientists stand on
high ladders,
taking down
God's marks
one by one.

And a tremendous glowing sun rises,
clearing space for
what?

Socrates nods his heavy old head.

Free

Trousers and a jacket
can feel very small
as I walk behind a new
yellow robe.

"Has your heart room for me?"

But wait! —
When the sunflower
laughs, and
the great red sun
bares her heart,
there is no "monk"
or "layman"!

Space

This open field

with yellow grass
    and darker trees
        around

I walk

my mind
    the clear sky itself
my body
    trees, grass, and soil

On This Earth

Who can say
that your path and mine
are different?

— when clouds
float softly across the sky,
sunrays play in
fields of dark and light! —

Next to this,
another image:

A boy is sitting on
the ground. The air
is burning, dry.
Flies are crawling
around his eyes,
all the way into
the corners.

With one eye dark
as the deep gorge,
I walk on;
my other eye sparkles
in sunlight.

The warmth of your hand
thaws the deep icicles.
What path can we take
that hearts may beat
freely again?

Morning

This early morning my chest
feels tender and soft.
A friend's kisses linger
on my right cheek, another's
tears on my left.
There is a great stillness
all around.

An ancient, deep dream
has come to mind.
As the iron thread bursts,
the flower comes into bloom.

Refuge

A slight smile on your lips
can change grouchiness & fear;
send energy to fingertips,
to nostrils, eyes and hair.

A calm & gentle breath
can help you see the way it is,
can change your attitude to death,
and give you insight into THIS!

Dandelion

Dandelion!
Lotus of the
industrial
age! You
make your
way through
pavements,
bloom in
backyards full of
old junk and on
polished lawns —
and carry no mark
of rusty iron or of

manicured bushes!
Your leaves are stiff
and shaggy, your taste
bitter and clear
(my liver enjoys it
a lot) — you are
uncombed and shining
like a hairy
little sun.
Well liked or
disliked, your
courage is intact,
your light
strong, not
blown about
by the eight worldly
winds —
until you use
them to secure
your rebirth in
10,000 new backyards
and gardens.
Han Shan of the pavement!
Backyard Milarepa! Fools
scowl at you; the
wise may
simply smile.

Sketch

What a wonderful web,
with a thousand strongly colored
threads vibrating in the winds.
Winds from East and North, Southwest
and every angle, swirl the
autumn leaves and spread them.
On the ocean, waves are
meeting, rising, sinking,
merging, parting...
A thousand people exchange
handshakes, a thousand thoughts
exchange their homes.
Here is nothing to hold
on to, nothing to let go of.

Reconciling with Christianity

Holding open the door for an elderly man at our neighborhood shopping center, I was met with this question: "Do you live your life for Jesus?" When I answered no, he told me that my life was without meaning. When I still couldn't agree, he firmly concluded, "You are Satan's child!" This small episode resonated with an old memory. I wasn't brought up in a very Christian home, my family finding God in nature rather than in church. Only at school did I learn stories of Jesus. So when the time came for my confirmation ceremony, I decided neither to take part in the ceremony nor the preparations. I took the question of belief seriously and felt it was wrong to profess a faith I didn't have. But our local pastor did not accept this, and he tried to force me, slandered me to my classmates, and made my already vulnerable teenage life even more difficult. Finally he phoned my mother and told her that I was doomed!

The churches — Protestant and Catholic — have a history of giving people guilt feelings, condemning groups like gays and lesbians and denouncing, or killing, unbelievers and heretics. Less than two hundred years ago, Shamans of Sami people ("Laplanders"), a small part of my ancestry, were lynched outside churches in Norway, their sacred drums burned, and Sami songs and even language banned for being pagan. It was easier for me to feel one with the victims of the Church than to feel that Christianity was part of my heritage.

Therefore, I was surprised at my strongly positive response to Thây's comments on the Sermon of the Mount. Was Christianity part of me after all? I started reading bridge builders like Fr. Enomiya Lasalle and Br. David Steindl-Rast, took part in dialogue, and even coordinated a Christian-Buddhist Zen retreat. I could appreciate the beauty of Rembrandt's portrait of Christ, Dostoyevsky's *The Brothers Karamazov,* as well as many of Christ's powerful sayings and many good, open-minded friends who found their foundation in their Christian faith. Still, I did not feel at home in churches, and instances of Christian narrow-mindedness still hurt. This somewhat uneasy situation lasted until Sister Annabel asked me to translate the Six Prostrations into Norwegian. Just reading them in *The Mindfulness Bell* didn't make such a strong impression, but working on the translation, I noticed my great resistance to seeing Christ and the Church as my spiritual ancestors. Something in me loudly cried "No!"

If it weren't for my strong commitment to Thây as my teacher, I might have turned away. Instead, I brought my dilemma into meditation and discovered rage and sorrow. All my reading and discussions with openhearted, undogmatic Christians hadn't been quite to the point, because the question really concerned the other aspect, the narrow-mindedness. By acknowledging my anger and hurt feelings, this knot began to dissolve, already a great relief, but it also became clear that my feelings have been similar to this verse in the *Dhammapada:* "Look how he abused me and beat me, how he threw me down and robbed me. Live with such thoughts and you live in hate."

With this starting point, it became possible to take a new, calm look at the abuses as well as the humanity of the Christian tradition. I can see how narrow-mindedness and thirst for power have their roots in fear of evil and death, strong wishes to be right and convince others, and, paradoxically, the inspiration from and love for a deep teacher like Christ. Of course, such elements are in me, too.

Reconciliation with Christianity may be difficult, for there are strong feelings involved — feelings we need to respect. Still, reconciliation is possible and rewarding. Difficulties with Christianity may have led to a distrust of "religion" that actually prevents us from embracing Buddhism fully — much as Sister Jina suggested in the Winter 1994 issue of *The Mindfulness Bell.* By working to understand and forgive the people who have hurt us in questions of religion, we can see our common humanity. We can see Jesus as a great teacher and understand the real spiritual and cultural value of the Christian faith. And we can have real communication with many Christians who also feel uneasy about abuses of their faith. By discovering our true relationship to Christianity, we may or may not find it to be our main spiritual root. In Norway, many people see nature as a great source of religious feelings — perhaps an inheritance from our old pre-Christian religion. But whatever we find, the search will make us more whole and enable us to feel more deeply. Otherwise, our spiritual practice may be too dry and intellectual.

O!

After discussing
    for hours, life, the Good,
        what we can do —

the words suddenly
    fall away
        & I see you

really

Calm

Clear autumn air
    on each side of
        a thin membrane

Sounds enveloped
    by great silence

Thoughts, feelings,
    a sore muscle:
        there's room enough

for all, nothing
    to make a fuss about

A Rose

Come, dear, & let us go
to the cave with no roof or walls,
taste the springwater of silence
& see the stars get lit & fade.
Let us sit on cushions of here & now,
& let a rose bloom
in open space.

Snow

Snow makes life
so beautiful!
Walking snowy streets,
with street lights
pointing to a creamy sky,
Western civilization almost
seems a good idea.

Childhood snow —
the realm of fantasy,
a kingdom to dig caves in —
caves for candles,
caves to sit in...
with darkness gathering
outside.

Snow for snowballs,
snow for rolling mindlessly around,
snow to fall in (on your skis),
and snow for eating (secretly,
out of sight of grown-ups).

And the sound of cold
weather: snow creaking
under your boots! Can you
feel this cold still, and the
half-terrified glee
when your tongue tip or finger
stuck for a moment to
a rail of cold iron!

Today, I walk in snow,
and the sight of
children building lanterns,
houses resting peacefully
under white, soft roofs,
gives calm
and quiet joy.

Sadness and the Sky

Being sad
about my illness
is part of me.

It doesn't hide
the blue sky, the
dancing clouds, or
your smile.

The Joy of Walking Fast

On July 22, 1997, I underwent open-heart surgery at Children's Hospital in Boston. Through the help of Barry Roth and Eurydice Hersey — old friends from Plum Village — and a lot of happy coincidences, I had got in touch with the hospital's clinic for adults with congenital heart disease. Before the surgery, I felt well-prepared: many friends all over the world had offered their support and our Sangha practiced the Five Remembrances for a few weeks in the spring. I had felt some guilt towards my wife and mother: what if I died during surgery? During the contemplation on death, I realized that it was outside of my control whether I would die or not. This was a relief.

The doctors and nurses at Children's were wonderful — real experts and also warm and caring. Still, the time after surgery was hard, much harder than I had expected. I experienced some difficulties, like a blood clot in my right leg; a long period of fever due to medicine allergy; and, of course, a lot of pain. Major surgery is a major strain on both body and mind. It's common for people who undergo open-heart surgery to feel depressed afterwards. This happened to me as well, especially after I was discharged from the safe womb of the hospital and we lived in an apartment in Cambridge near the hospital but far away from home. Happily, the longest period of depression lasted only half a day, but depressed periods recurred intensely and frequently. I cried and cried. Eevi was the most wonderful support, just being there for me without trying to change my reactions. I could never have managed without her! Many long-distance phone calls to my mother and other relatives and friends in Norway were encouraging too.

It felt good to know that many friends were thinking of us, praying for us, giving financial support... Warm thanks to you all! Jørgen and Katla Hannibal were our "information centre" in Europe; being there for all who wanted to know how things were going. In the Boston area, Candace Cassin helped us with many practical things, besides keeping Eevi company at the time of surgery and visiting us a lot — both at the hospital and in the difficult time afterwards. Elizabeth Wood found time in a hectic schedule to find an apartment for us, and lent us her car for three weeks! She also introduced us to the Boston Sangha. From the summer retreat in Plum Village there came a lovely poster with a beautiful drawing and greetings from many dear friends. I cried while reading it, but not from depression! So many people offered support in some ways — I'd like to mention everyone, but it would probably fill the whole book.

My surgery was extremely successful. Already after a few days, my oxygen levels had increased dramatically. According to Eevi, I walked faster than ever before. Now, seven weeks later, my blood is even more rich in oxygen. I feel stronger day by day, although I still need time and exercise to reap the fruits of surgery fully. It's amazing not to be out of breath and tired from doing common, "normal" activities, and I enjoy this "non-toothache." Just a simple thing like walking fast gives tremendous joy. Before surgery, someone said, "Now, you'll maybe be able to understand those who find (slow) walking meditation difficult!" Time will tell; it's enough for me to enjoy being able to walk fast (and run, when the pain and stiff muscles in my chest and shoulders disappear)... However I'm sure that I'll understand people with depression better. The people who were simply able to listen, having room for my situation as it was, were of much greater help than those who gave lots of advice or tried to make things sound better than they were. In theory, I knew this already — but I forget too easily. Now, I really know, and that makes all the difference. I regret all the situations where I haven't been able just to listen to people's sorrows but have tried to persuade them to feel different.

Did my mindfulness practice help me through this difficult time? Some nurses said I healed as quickly as the little kids... Otherwise, it's hard to say; the practice is so much part of me that I can't imagine life without it. It certainly didn't spare me pain and tears, but I think I lived more in the present and was able to enjoy the moments of no hardships — and go fully into the difficult times. At times, I felt I should be more brave, calm, etc., but Eevi wisely told me I didn't need to be other than I am. It's easy to use one's self-image as "a practitioner" to deny one's experience, instead of being open to what's there. To trust nature to take a good course if we don't interfere with ideas of how it should be — that's perhaps the greatest faith. How good to have friends who can remind us!

Still, Alive

On a high bed
in a white room
I lie and
am alive.
My heartbeats are
mirrored on a TV-screen.
Light curtains are
animated by a breeze.

In the corridors
outside, men and women
walk in bathrobes,
their faces tired, lit
by the pale light of patience.

What is important?
To be free from pain, to
have a hand to hold, or
to draw another breath?

Outside again,
the sky is larger and clearer
than before, and the birch tree
has leaves of pure gold.

Mindfulness of the Body

Our bodies can bring us joy and pain, triumph and defeat, contentment and craving. We spend a lot of time getting our bodies "in shape" — through sports, health regimes, and beauty treatments, but somehow, they never seem to be enough. Living too fast and in unnatural environments, we become too easily estranged from just experiencing our bodies, and we become victims of the ideal of the perfect body as is marketed by the popular press, films, TV, and advertising.

Since real bodies aren't idealized, having this idea of perfection creates a split in us. We struggle to reach it and we push away our feelings of failure. Huge industries of cosmetics, fashion, and workout studios bear witness to this, as does the sinister increase in eating disorders and cosmetic surgery. We are in conflict with ourselves.

In the *Sutra on the Four Establishments of Mindfulness,* the Buddha offers a different way. This discourse is the classic catalog of mindfulness exercises, and about half of them deal with awareness of breathing and the body, which is also a door to knowing feelings, mind, and world.

Through being aware of our breathing and the positions and movements of our bodies, we unite body and mind and return to the present moment. We learn to live *in* our bodies and become intimate with ourselves on a deep level. We can reach a greater stability and calm, because we no longer are at the mercy of speedily changing ideas and feelings. We learn to experience what it means to be, rather than only experience ideas about being. As Stephen Levine has said, having an in-the-body experience is much more valuable than having an out-of-body experience!

At times, this can be difficult, since we store many old feelings and judgments in our bodies and our breathing. By giving attention to our bodies, we get to know these feelings and "internal knots" as well — and they are not always pleasant! So we practice mindfulness of the body with utmost kindness. When meditating on the body, we may become aware of thoughts or feelings like, "My breathing is too shallow," "Who will ever love me when I'm so skinny (fat, tall, short, etc.)?", or "I'll never get enlightened with this terrible posture!" But we don't practice mindfulness to change ourselves in accord with some preconceived idea, and we don't have to believe thoughts like these. We only want to know ourselves — body and soul — and we don't need to strive toward any specific idea. By being open, kind, and aware, slowly expanding our understanding, we open for transformation to take place at deeper levels than our surface consciousness.

Transformation is a process of nature. We just need to tend the garden of our body and soul, let in sun and fresh air, and give attention and affection to the many small creatures who live there. Then, nature itself will take care of our transformation. In fact, we *are* nature, much larger than our mind and body, and mindfulness of body can show us this. It shows that bodily sensations and impulses — as well as our thoughts, memories, and feelings — largely have their own life as natural beings. We need to spend a long time to befriend them and tame them (as Saint-Exupéry says in *The Little Prince*, to tame *is* to befriend). Attention and kindness are more useful than opinions, force, or willpower.

There are specific exercises that can help us see our connection to nature. By being aware that the four elements of fire, water, air, and earth are in us and everywhere around us, we can transcend feelings and images of isolation. It is curious that *images* of the body, often at a semiconscious level, can feel much more isolated than the actual *experience* of body-in-surroundings. At certain times in life, contemplating our body as a rotting corpse can help us see that our body also has a part in nature's cycle of decay and new growth.

Mindfulness of body can be our great teacher in trusting nature — the nature of both body and soul. Trust, not because nature will never give us suffering, but because the ultimate, sacred dimension can be found right here. This offers deep healing on levels we may only be dimly aware of at the moment.

In the Japanese Garden

Yellow autumn bamboo, ferns
an unpainted gate

Around each bend, behind each tree
something new appears

half hidden
half visible

By walking you are inside
the garden, you create the garden

Can you see? Only a receptive
open mind

takes part in the garden
anew... anew

each step more quiet
each feeling calmer

floating in open space
inside you? around you?

Mother

I sense something
    missing

Something important

And suddenly
    I see

It's mother
Mother is no longer here

I'll never hear her voice
    again
Never see her liveliness, her
    vitality, her
joy — or her sorrow & pain...

She has peace now.
Resting at the source.

More & more I see
 how remarkable
    she was; how open & direct
        generous & righteous
            caring — & angry at injustice
wise

Her whole life
        she gave
                her whole being. To me
& many others.

So much of what I understand
    of life
        of death
  stems from her.

So much of who I am
    stems from her.

That is good.
We love each other.
She is resting now.

Astrid Myreng,
Source of Courageous Engagement

January 5, 1926 — October 27, 1997

The greatest loss of my life has happened:
Mother died. She taught me so much about life
and death, helped me through many times of
painful or life-threatening illness. A fiercely
engaged person, she worked against social
injustices and environmental destruction. She
left me a valuable heritage: her love of literature
and nature; a fearless openness in expressing
views and feelings and dealing with difficulties;
and genuine care for other people — so many
have been touched by her life.

She had little interest in possessions. Once,
by accident, she threw her diamond ring in the
garbage and was unable to retrieve it. Before
long, she relished this incident as a good story.
She was so alive!

We had no "unfinished business" — the last
thing we said to each other was that we loved
each other. She died suddenly and painlessly at
four in the morning. Her last words were: "I
know I am dying, and I wish to die." She had
seen her two great hopes come true: I had
married Eevi a year and a half earlier and my
recent surgery in Boston had given me the

strength she always hoped for. Her greatest desire was for my happiness.

In her later years, she became very fond of Buddhism, through Thây's books which I read for her, and through meeting and housing monks, nuns, and lay teachers who visited Norway. She was amused by imagining what the neighbors might think when exotic-looking people came to our flat.

Brother Doji transmitted the Refuges to her during her funeral and gave her the Dharma name "Source of Courageous Engagement." We created a traditional Norwegian ceremony but with Buddhist elements, and received many positive, even grateful, comments. This was a worthy conclusion for a life of great engagement. She was a bodhisattva. What efforts I make in the Dharma, to a great extent, stem from her. I miss her so much!

POEMS FOR EEVI

For You

The light of your face
    your fingertips
        light against my hand — &

your words
    clear water in moss
        breeze
    fluttering leaves

two hearts meet
bathing in light
so easy —
    & so brave
so tender
so beautiful

    peace
sunshine deep in water
    & small raindrops
        that
            glitter

Our Path

The gifts you give me
are like the sun, rain, & golden plums;
overflow of peace and joy.
You give me so much, so boundlessly much;
not only when you know you give, but
by being you, by sharing
your sorrow as well as your joy.
I love *all* of you.

My path has become our path.

My practice is to give you happiness — & to be
open to all the happiness that I receive
from you, my love. My vow is to
do all that I can to be the one you need;
the one who has room for your sorrows,
who can share your joys; who can ask
for help when needed.

Our path is the path of love, a path in openness
& truth.

When I fail — & I know it happens
all too often — I will always ask you to forgive, &
trust in your love. With this trust,
I will open my heart more & more, &
learn how to be the one you need.

Our path embraces life. Together, there's
nothing we can't do!

Joy

You know —
    I found out —

When the poets say
    love,
they mean
    longing

But
my heart
    is filled
        with light
streams of
    pure joy!

Love is you
    your voice
        eyes
            lips
the whole, living you

Light meets light
so the galaxies pale
    & thoughts flow
        on exulting
            streams
                of
                JOY!

Today

Today
the words fell out of their books.
Piles of letters landed
like dust on the floor, while
the pages were left empty.

Yes!
For how could
    the learned works
catch the light
    that was lit
       in your eyes
— & in my heart —

a glittering world
    of joy and tenderness

Suddenly

    LIFE

is poetry

Parallax Press publishes books and tapes on Buddhism and related subjects to make them accessible and alive for contemporary readers. It is our hope that doing so will help alleviate suffering and create a more peaceful world.

We carry all books and tapes by Thich Nhat Hanh. For a copy of our free catalog, please write to:

Parallax Press
P.O. Box 7355
Berkeley, California 94707
www.parallax.org